BETTY FRIEDAN

by Susan Taylor-Boyd

For a free color catalog describing Gareth Stevens' list of high-quality children's books, call 1-800-341-3569 (USA) or 1-800-461-9120 (Canada).

Picture Credits

American Institute of Physics, Niels Bohr Library, Lande Collection — 17 (lower); The Bettmann Archive — 15, 19 (both); map by Sharon Burris, © Gareth Stevens, Inc. — 60; © Diana Mara Henry 1978 — 54 (upper); Historical Pictures Service, Chicago, Illinois — 22; Lake County Museum, Curt Teich Postcard Archives, Wauconda, Illinois — 7, 9, 10, 11, 21, 24, 28, 29, 57 (upper); © Bettye Lane — 4, 32, 59; National Organization for Women — 36, 37, 44, 46, 48, 54 (lower); James Oberg Archive — 56; © Tom Redman, 1990, cover; The Schlesinger Library, Radcliffe College — 6 (both), 12, 13, 14, 20, 26, 30; UPI/Bettmann Newsphotos — 17 (upper), 35, 38, 40, 47 (lower); Wide World Photos, Inc. — 45, 47 (upper), 50, 52, 57 (lower), 58.

A Gareth Stevens Children's Books edition

Edited, designed, and produced by
Gareth Stevens Children's Books
RiverCenter Building, Suite 201
1555 North RiverCenter Drive
Milwaukee, Wisconsin 53212, USA

Library of Congress Cataloging-in-Publication Data

Taylor-Boyd, Susan, 1949-
    Betty Friedan / by Susan Taylor-Boyd.
       p. cm. — (People who have helped the world)
    Summary: Follows the life and work of the feminist who wrote "The Feminine Mystique" and helped found the National Organization for Women.
    ISBN 0-8368-0104-0
    1. Friedan, Betty — Juvenile literature. 2. Feminists — United States — Biography — Juvenile literature. [1. Friedan, Betty. 2. Feminists.] I. Title. II. Series.
HQ1413.F75T39 1990   305.42'092—dc20
[B]   [92]   90-9691

Series conceived by Helen Exley
Series editor: Rhoda Irene Sherwood
Editor/research editor: Tom Barnett
Research editor: John D. Rateliff
Picture editor: Daniel Helminak
Layout: Kristi Ludwig
Copy editor: Scott Enk
Editorial assistant: Diane Laska

Printed in the United States of America

1 2 3 4 5 6 7 8 9 96 95 94 93 92 91 90

BETTY FRIEDAN

Voice for women's rights, advocate of human rights

by Susan Taylor-Boyd

Gareth Stevens Children's Books
MILWAUKEE

An unhappy legacy

"Look at these unpaid bills," Harry Goldstein stormed at his wife, Miriam. "You just can't keep spending like this."

"I want to make our house a place I . . . we . . . can be proud of. Is that such a crime? This is what I do well. Please don't tell me I have to stop," Miriam sobbed. "You have your jewelry store. I have the house and the children. I can't just sit around all day. I have to do *something*."

Their oldest daughter, Betty, felt so confused. She hated listening to their fights. "Please, God, make them stop," she would whisper to herself.

She knew her mother was unhappy, but why? The large, comfortable home of the Goldsteins stood as one of the more envied houses in Peoria, Illinois. Every few months she would redecorate, repainting walls or changing the window dressings. The bookcases and end tables held beautiful porcelain figurines. The house was always immaculate. Wherever guests looked, they found elegance and beauty.

Even during the Great Depression, when many families had no money for food or rent, Miriam kept her home and her children in the latest styles. Harry tolerated Miriam's spending because he could usually afford it. But as the economy became worse and worse, Harry began to see the unpaid bills growing. Miriam would have to learn to cut back! He also didn't realize that to recoup money she'd spent on furnishings rather than necessities, Miriam had begun to gamble.

By 1932, as the depression was worsening, Betty Goldstein was eleven. Nearly every night she would be awakened by her parents' fighting. Sometimes the fights were about the children. Sometimes they were about how much time Harry spent at the store. But usually the fights were about money.

"In almost every marriage there is a selfish and an unselfish partner. A pattern is set up and soon becomes inflexible, of one person always making the demands and one person always giving way."

Iris Murdoch,
English novelist

Top: Harry Goldstein encouraged Betty to go to college and to have a career. His attitude was unusual for the 1940s.

Above: Miriam Horwitz Goldstein grew bored with her work at home. Once a reporter herself, she encouraged Betty to write.

Even though her father didn't know about Miriam's gambling, Betty did. "Don't you dare tell your father," Miriam would plead when Betty learned of another loss. Betty promised, even though she hated keeping secrets from her father. But still she wondered: Why couldn't her mother be happy with what she had? Why was she always looking for something else?

Twenty-five years later, when Betty had her own family, she began to understand. Her husband was a successful advertising executive. They had a beautiful home and three healthy children. But Betty was miserable, and she was angry. She couldn't figure out the reason. She seemed to be living her mother's life, and she hated that. Then she realized that one reason she felt miserable was that she felt guilty about feeling miserable! She guessed Miriam must have felt this, too. So many women didn't have husbands to help pay the bills and raise their children. Betty and her mother should feel lucky to have their seemingly perfect lives. If we are unhappy, she thought, then maybe we are just ungrateful.

In the next few years, Betty would learn from neighbors, friends, and college classmates that they were unhappy too. Many of them had the same good fortune as Betty and her mother. What could be wrong? Why were so many women unhappy with their lives?

In search of an answer

Betty went in search of an answer. This search changed her from a shy, easily embarrassed young woman to an outspoken campaigner for women's rights. She began by listening to what women thought. Then, in 1963, her book *The Feminine Mystique* appeared. This ground-breaking book expressed the unhappiness of women, especially married women, and suggested some reasons for the unhappiness. Reading this book, women learned that they weren't alone in feeling dissatisfied with their lives.

In time, Betty helped create lasting solutions to the problems women faced in achieving independence and equality. She organized committees to present employment issues to government at the state and federal level. She worked to open up "male only" jobs for women and to improve women's pay.

Out of these efforts came the idea of creating a nationwide organization of feminist women and men. In 1966, Betty and some other feminists formed this group — the National Organization for Women. From this, in 1971, grew the National Women's Political Caucus. She also continued to write — in 1976, she published *It Changed My Life: Writings on the Women's Movement*, and, in 1981, *The Second Stage*.

In addition to her writing, Betty traveled to promote women's issues and women's rights. She was invited to other countries to help people discuss issues affecting women and to help the people use political and legal means to improve conditions for women. In 1975, she promoted the first international women's conference, in Mexico. In 1977, she helped organize the first National Women's Conference, in Houston, Texas. She also traveled all over America speaking out in favor of the Equal Rights Amendment (ERA). This constitutional amendment would have guaranteed legal equality for all people in America, regardless of sex.

Today, Betty continues to speak out on women's issues. As a grandmother, she's begun exploring the problems older women face, such as losing their husbands and having little income. She is presently writing a book about these issues.

"My mother's like a rock that's been smoothed by a wave, like a void. She's put so much into her family that there's nothing left, and she resents us because she doesn't get enough in return."
A seventeen-year-old girl writing to Friedan, quoted in Friedan's book It Changed My Life

"In politics, if you want anything said, ask a man; if you want anything done, ask a woman."
Margaret Thatcher, prime minister of Great Britain

This ad from 1916 suggests the standard of beauty for women of Miriam Goldstein's generation.

"Why?"

All this political activism began in Betty's own home, in her own life. She began her quest in order to find out why her mother and she were so miserable. By asking why, she was able to discover some truths about the condition of women in our society; women needed choices and the freedom to pursue those choices; women with children needed day-care services; women needed training and education for better-paying jobs. In time she learned these were merely partial answers. Miriam had had money and education but still couldn't get out of the rut women so often fell into. What was this problem that had no name?

A mismatched couple

Before Miriam Horwitz married Harry Goldstein in 1920, she had very happily worked as a reporter of social events for the local newspaper in Peoria, Illinois. She was also a college graduate. Harry, who had quit school at thirteen, began a small business which grew into a thriving jewelry store in Peoria.

Friends thought that Miriam and Harry did not have very much in common. Harry was a relatively uneducated emigrant from Germany, while Miriam was the daughter of a prominent local physician. Harry was forty years old, Miriam only twenty-three. The only thing they seemed to have in common was that they were Jewish. But Miriam recognized Harry's solid business sense and his love for her. At first that seemed enough to make a good marriage.

The only problem was that Miriam didn't want to give up her job reporting social events. At this time it was expected, however, that women would stay home and devote themselves to their homes and families if their husbands earned enough money to support them. So Miriam became a housewife.

Unhappy at home

A year after the marriage, on February 4, 1921, Miriam gave birth to Betty. In 1922, a daughter, Amy, followed, then Harry, Jr.

Miriam loved her children, but she was also restless. Harry was gone all day at the store, and she was left at home with three children. No longer did she have the welcome distractions and excitement of the other reporters at the newspaper, the parties she would attend and report on, and the demands of a deadline. There was always work to do around the house, but most of it did not require her college education. Miriam wasn't challenged. She also began to think it was unfair that she was not using her education. She began to resent Harry's business success.

To compensate, Miriam tried to turn her energies toward volunteer work — an acceptable way for wives to work outside the home. She taught Sunday school and participated in Hadassah and the Temple Sisterhood (two Jewish women's groups that did volunteer work in the community). She also played bridge in the afternoon with friends. But these activities were not enough to overcome her great unhappiness.

Soon Miriam's dissatisfaction began affecting the entire family. Betty watched her mother grow more and more resentful of her life. Soon, besides overspending to make herself feel better, Miriam began to criticize Harry in public. She began to demand perfection from her children and raged if things weren't done

Well-off married women rarely held outside employment. Some of these women donated their energy and money to the arts or to civic projects. The Ladies Club of Miami, Florida, was responsible for the construction of this city library.

LADIES CLUB AND LIBRARY, MIAMI, FLA.

9

Peoria, where Betty grew up, was a beautiful, growing city, even during the Great Depression. The city's economy wasn't totally dependent on farming or on steel manufacturing, two industries badly affected by the depression. So the citizens of Peoria had some economic difficulty, but not as much as people in other parts of the country.

the way she expected. All this anger and criticism confused Betty, Amy, and Harry, Jr.

Harry, however, cheered the children and continued to support them. He encouraged them to do well in school because he knew that a lack of education could hold them back. Betty loved to read, so her father would take her to the library every Saturday. He also encouraged his children to be creative.

In her way, so did Miriam. She criticized the children more than Harry, but she also made sure they were exposed to cultural events. Whenever a play or musical came to Peoria, she was the one who got tickets for the family. Betty soon developed a love for the theater. And later, when Betty began to take an interest in writing, she would also get her mother's encouragement. Perhaps it was because of this support that she was baffled when her mother lashed out in anger or criticized her unfairly.

Doing it her way

Betty hated Peoria. No one there seemed to accept her. In elementary school, the fact that she was Jewish never seemed to matter. But as she grew older, as much as she wanted to fit in at high school, she wasn't allowed to join the clubs for girls, or the popular cliques. In many ways she was unlike the children she went to school with. Her Jewish faith and her exotic

Skyline from East Bluff, Peoria, Ill.

10

features set her apart and caused some children to make fun of her. No matter how smart or how well-to-do she was, she wasn't accepted.

Betty decided that her classmates shouldn't be the ones to decide how she should act. At first she had tried to hide her intelligence because she thought that would make the boys notice her. But she still was ignored. Finally one day she decided it was time to be the way she wanted to be. "If they don't like me, then someday, by God, they're going to respect me." Rather than hide her intelligence, Betty decided to be proud of it. In her junior year at Central High, she signed up for chemistry, algebra, Latin, French, and English, a very difficult schedule. She spoke out in class. And she began to participate in school activities.

Stepping into the spotlight

Once in elementary school, she had formed a club with her friends called the "Baddy Baddy." On Betty's signal the students would disrupt the classroom by coughing loudly or dropping their books. One day, the principal called her in. He said, "You've got a talent for leadership, Betty, but why do you use it to do harm? I hope you find a way to use it wisely." Years

"Her nose is long, her hair, despite patient attention at the beauty parlor, often askew. Nothing fits the accepted model of beauty. Yet she exerts a powerful, haunting attractiveness — that special combustion that lights up a few rare individuals interacting with their audience."

An editor describing Betty Friedan, as quoted in Marcia Cohen's The Sisterhood

A cartoon from 1945 implying that intelligence was unattractive in women. For a while, Betty thought that she would be more popular if she pretended not to be intelligent.

Betty's senior picture in her high school yearbook. The description of her school activities reads:
"GOLDSTEIN, BETTYE Opinion Staff, Tide Staff, Charvice, Junior National Honor Society, 'Jane Eyre,' Jusendra, French Club, Cue Club, Quill and Scroll, Social Science Club."
She would later drop the e from her name.

later she remembered these words. She could be a leader and make positive changes.

Betty auditioned for school plays and found some acceptance on the stage. Normally she was very shy, but on stage she could hide behind a character and be as bold as she wanted.

Once she played the madwoman in a production of Charlotte Bronte's novel *Jane Eyre.* Her insane laughter as she made her entrance shook the audience with fright and earned her a special ovation. Years later, although still very shy, she would fall back on her dramatic training to help her make speeches.

Betty also inherited Miriam's love of writing. Writing was an area where mother and daughter could get along and work together. Miriam felt flattered that Betty took such a serious interest in writing, and this allowed them to discuss something besides Miriam's criticisms of Betty's appearance.

Betty did book reviews for *Opinion,* the school newspaper, and wrote poems for herself. Then she decided that the school needed a literary magazine, so with Miriam's encouragement she started one called *Tide.* She raised the money for printing and selected the literary entries for each issue. The magazine was a big success at school.

Betty's English teacher, Miss Crowder, also recognized Betty's writing skills and encouraged her to put them to use. She showed Betty how to develop her own style of writing and how to select better books to read. She also encouraged Betty to expand the scope of her reading to include essays and poetry. As Betty read various essayists, she began to realize how much power and persuasion a piece of writing could have. She decided that writing would be a good way to express ideas that she felt were important.

So she began to express her own opinions through writing. Students loved her column, "Cabbages and Kings," in the school paper. In it, she would discuss different issues affecting school or student life. Her essay in a contest using the topic "Why I Am Proud to Be an American" won first prize. Betty began to find all the power and acceptance she had been looking for in school through her writing. She knew that she would never stop writing.

New dreams

The high school sororities still would not admit her because she was Jewish, but in every other aspect of high school Betty achieved her goal of respect and acceptance. Still, the sting of anti-Semitism, prejudice against her because she was Jewish, would affect her beliefs and sense of fairness all her life. She came to realize that no one should be ignored or discriminated against for any reason.

Religion wasn't the only object of discrimination, she discovered. Race, physical disabilities, poverty, lack of education, and gender — all were targets for prejudice. This eventually helped her to figure out why her mother was so unhappy. The fact that Miriam was a woman limited her choices. Her education and her professional experience didn't give Miriam any more choices about what to do with her life. She was expected to be a wife and mother.

Betty's insights were slow to come. In high school, she still believed that a woman's *ultimate* goal was to make a good marriage. She often prayed at night: "I want a boy who will love me best, and I want a work to do." Even her senior essay reflected this wish. The prayer Betty had whispered to herself privately, she now made public: "I want to fall in love and be loved and be needed by someone. I want to have children."

Quill and Scroll, Betty's writing club. She is in the center of the first row.

"No one can make you feel inferior without your consent."
Eleanor Roosevelt

13

But Betty had learned something watching her mother's bitterness and feeling its effects. She might not yet know why, but she knew her prayer had been too limited. She was beginning to realize that "a work to do" meant something of importance beyond a husband and a family.

As important as raising a family was, she thought, it was in many ways short-term. Women needed to continue the educational challenge they took up in high school and college. They needed to have goals beyond the family. She was beginning to understand her mother's frustration.

So her senior essay continued, "I know this. I don't want to marry a man and keep house for him and be the mother of his children and nothing else. I want to *do* something with my life. I want success and fame."

WAR!

The year was 1938. Betty was seventeen and about to graduate from high school. In Germany, the Nazis were putting their anti-Semitic programs into practice. Families were separated, and people were imprisoned, tortured, and killed because of their religious beliefs. It was a time of great political and social upheaval. Soon millions of young men her own age would be going off to war, and women would be called on to take the men's places in the work force. For Betty, it was an explosive time to form her ideas about the world.

But for the moment, getting out of Peoria monopolized Betty's interest. She had been accepted at Smith College, an exclusive women's college in western Massachusetts. Finally, Betty could leave both the town she hated and an increasingly unhappy family.

As Miriam saw her responsibilities as a mother coming to an end, she desperately began to increase her manipulation of her children. She reminded Betty, for instance, that she was the ugly sister while Amy was the pretty one. Then she reminded Amy that Betty was more intelligent. Perhaps Miriam thought that her comparisons would motivate the girls. In fact, the competition hurt Betty and Amy, and they have never developed a close relationship.

Harry was happy to see his "bookworm" daughter so successful. Sometimes he had worried that she was

Opposite: Shy and afraid of speaking in front of large crowds, Betty loved acting. A friend once told Betty that she looked like the famous actress Bette Davis. Here Friedan strikes a pose similar to those Davis did for her publicity photos.

When Adolf Hitler became chancellor of Germany in 1933, many foreign leaders seemed unconcerned about the threat to other European countries. The United States tried to stay out of the conflict. Friedan wrote many editorials urging Americans to get involved. She worried about Hitler's anti-Jewish policies and his desire to take over countries in Europe that were not able to defend themselves against his army.

too smart, *too* studious. But he quickly realized that studying made her happy. He wished Miriam could find an outlet, but by now their relationship had become bitter. It was too late for Miriam, he thought, but he hoped Betty would find a better way to live.

Off to school

Betty began college in September 1938. Smith was everything she had hoped it would be. She quickly found that most of the women liked her for what she had to offer. Her ideas excited them and her enthusiasm for political discussion impressed them. In high school most of the girls only wanted to talk about boys, but at Smith the topics were politics, religion, and social issues. She did notice, however, that there was anti-Semitism which limited the clubs she could join.

But Betty also found that the women and professors at Smith were questioning their own prejudices. In high school she had written an essay about Adolf Hitler, the German dictator. She questioned whether his policies of murder and terror could ever be put into practice in the democratic atmosphere of America.

Now she found many others in America asking the same thing. For years some people had quietly hated the Jews in America, and no one had seriously challenged that hatred. Now Hitler was proposing that Jews be placed in prison camps. And the news from Europe was that the concentration camps were really death camps. Betty had never imagined that prejudice could have such an ugly outcome.

In addition, many Jewish intellectuals, such as Albert Einstein, were escaping from central Europe and seeking jobs in the United States. These men and women were the foremost experts in their fields, especially the natural and social sciences. One of these areas was psychology, and Betty found herself drawn to it. Perhaps she could figure out why her mother was so unhappy and why anyone could hate groups of people because of their religion, skin color, or ideas.

Speaking out

Betty continued to develop her love of writing at Smith. She joined the American Student Union, an organization that opposed the policies of Hitler and the

Italian fascist dictator, Benito Mussolini. The union had a paper called *Focus*. Betty contributed poems and book reviews.

One book she reviewed, John Steinbeck's *Grapes of Wrath*, was a novel about the loss of farmland to drought and about farmers who were forced to move to California in search of a better life. She called it "a fiery document of protest." That book also increased her interest in the problems of working people — an interest that she would later combine with writing.

Betty also helped found the *Smith College Monthly*, a literary magazine. Through this magazine, she discovered a wider audience for her views on the events in Europe. When Hitler invaded Czechoslovakia, Poland, and France, Betty wrote passionate editorials. She told the readers that this kind of dictatorship and religious and racial hatred could develop even in the United States. She cautioned readers to think about their own prejudices and to guard against this senseless hatred that was tearing Europe apart.

Betty's writing once again brought her acceptance and the power to publicly express her opinions. Soon she became the editor of the college newspaper, *SCAN*. Now, twice a week, Betty had a forum to express her

Despite the lessons of World War II, even today, groups such as the Ku Klux Klan spread hatred against minorities.

World-renowned scientist Albert Einstein left Germany in 1933 and eventually immigrated to the United States.

ideas about labor, social inequalities, prejudice, and war. Even though her editorials were often harsh, people enjoyed them and paid attention because she wrote them so well. Once she tried to expose a secret society of young women that she felt dominated the social decisions on campus. But the college president thought the topic was too explosive and told Betty to kill the story. She did, but she also got in the last word. When that edition of the paper came out, she ran a blank page stamped in black — "CENSORED."

Choosing a path

Betty continued to pursue her degree in psychology, but she also began to explore other areas of study. She wanted to find a career where she could both explore new territory and write about that exploration. Her mother's job as a reporter, even though she only wrote about social events, proved to be a strong influence toward Betty's decision to become a writer.

Betty loved psychology, but it now seemed too narrow a field to contain all the interests she wanted to pursue. And psychology had a professional language all its own that most people couldn't understand. She wanted to reach the public, not push it away. Reporting for a newspaper, as her mother had, seemed like the best way to reach a large audience.

Many people influenced her through this soul-searching. Kurt Koffka, a leading psychologist of the 1930s and 1940s, was one of Betty's teachers at Smith. His enthusiasm for psychology had led her to make it her major.

At the same time she studied the history of Western civilization and American history. She discovered that even at a women's college, all the major historical figures studied were men. On her own she began to read about Elizabeth Cady Stanton, a founder of the women's rights convention held in Seneca Falls, New York, in 1848, and Susan B. Anthony, a strong supporter of women's right to vote. She realized that many women had fought for her right to express herself. Yet they were neglected in history books.

For two summers, Betty went away to continue her education. In 1940, she went to Iowa to study with Kurt Lewin. He was a well known psychologist who had

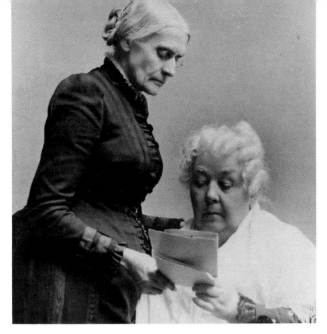

Susan B. Anthony (left) and Elizabeth Cady Stanton (right), two early leaders in the struggle for women's rights.

escaped from Germany as the oppression increased there. Lewin thought Betty had an excellent analytical and questioning mind and recognized her ability to dig beneath the surface of issues.

Equally impressive was her ability to see issues in a large context — that is, to apply what she learned to other areas. He encouraged her to earn a graduate degree in psychology. The next summer, in 1941, Betty went to the Highlander Folk School in Tennessee. Here people gathered to study the history of labor and the history of union organizing.

The goal of the school was to train people to educate others about the status of blue-collar workers and to promote labor reforms. Reporting on labor issues for newspapers was one way of accomplishing the school's goals. Betty began to combine her political passions, her interest in psychology, and her need to write.

Well-known German psychologist Kurt Lewin recognized Betty's talent and determination. Lewin encouraged Betty to continue her education and study psychology in graduate school.

Love won't wait

Betty now reached a crossroads. In June 1942, she would graduate from Smith. She could either find a man to marry or she could continue her education in psychology. She decided to apply to the University of California at Berkeley. With her excellent grades and strong recommendations, Berkeley accepted her.

But there was another problem to deal with. Betty became more and more unsure about psychology as her career choice. She found it intellectually interesting, but she didn't think it could really make any changes. Instead psychology always seemed to be voicing ideas or theories about events that had already happened rather than working to change their outcome. After a year at Berkeley, Betty knew psychology wasn't for her. So when Berkeley offered her a fellowship to work on a doctoral degree, Betty turned it down. She needed to be a doer rather than a theorist. Writing seemed to be a way to make things happen.

The decision to leave her studies and begin a career as a writer had been complicated. Besides Betty's doubts about psychology, she'd also fallen in love with a young man at Berkeley. She based part of her decision to refuse the fellowship on him. He would not be able to continue his studies, and he suggested that if she wanted to remain with him, she would have to quit. In the 1940s, a woman was expected to get married, have children, and follow her husband around as his career developed. It seemed natural to Betty to give up her academic goals for a young man.

An unhappy choice

But within days of refusing the fellowship, Betty suffered a severe asthma attack. These attacks would plague her with every tense, unhappy decision of her life. She knew that she should never have ignored her own feelings. Instead, she should have made a decision based entirely on what she felt was best for her. She knew she had to find something important and stimulating to do, so she left California and went to New York City to pursue a career as a writer.

Scared and still unsure about her decision to turn down the grant, Betty moved to New York in 1943. World War II continued, and there were few young men to fill all the jobs. Women found themselves in demand, so Betty was sure she'd find a job. She decided to focus on the newspapers. Whenever she thought about her happiest times in high school and in college, they were always when she worked on the paper. After only one day, she was hired as a labor reporter with the Federated Press. For the first time, her experience as a

Betty in 1942, the year she graduated from Smith College.

writer and her interest in labor issues and reporting were combined in one challenging position.

A breath of fresh air

In New York, her asthma improved. Her job with Federated Press challenged her, and she had renewed contact with several friends from Smith who also lived in the city. She and a few of these women found an apartment in a lively area in the middle of New York City. Betty loved her job. The only unhappiness in her life was her father's death in 1943. "Of overwork," Betty would tell her friends. She knew how hard Harry had worked to earn money to maintain the family's comfortable home and way of life.

World War II now drew to a close, promising new vitality in her social life as the soldiers returned home. While Betty and her friends rejoiced at the thought of all those single men coming back to the city, they also knew that these same men would be wanting their jobs back. During the war many women had been asked to fill the jobs men left to become soldiers. Suddenly women were needed to build airplanes, oversee companies, construct roads, and do all the other jobs that had been traditionally considered "men only."

Because many of the women were mothers, businesses established day-care centers so these women could be free to work. For four years these women had

Even in the 1940s, New York already had huge skyscrapers. Betty moved there in 1943 and began working as a reporter for the Federated Press, a wire service.

"What do women want?"
Sigmund Freud, founder
of psychoanalysis

21

experienced the challenge of handling a job, caring for a family, and managing a household. There had been stresses, certainly, but most women gladly took on the responsibility because they were helping their country in a time of need.

Gone — but not forgotten

The more the women worked, the more they realized they could handle jobs men had always said were too hard for women. They also learned that they enjoyed the independence, challenge, and companionship their jobs gave them. When the men came home in 1945, some of the women who had filled their positions were forced to give them up and return home. But the economy was so strong and production levels so high as a result of the war that many of the women, about four out of five, were able to keep working. The jobs they most often held, however, were those traditionally thought of as appropriate for women, jobs as secretaries, waitresses, or telephone operators.

Many of the women who did give up their jobs didn't lose their desire for outside employment or the confidence that they could handle it. They also began to question the traditional expectation that women become housewives.

Betty felt pressure to step aside for the returning soldiers. One day her superior came to her with the news that the young man who had held her job before he went into the army now wanted it back. Betty suddenly found herself unemployed. But unlike many other women, she didn't have a husband who could support her. She had only herself to depend upon. Worse, many of her friends and roommates were marrying, which only made Betty panic more.

How would she support herself? She had been taught that marriage meant security. And she certainly felt very insecure at that moment. No job. No husband. The asthma attacks returned. Fortunately, she was able to find another job as a labor reporter, but that only eased half of her anxiety.

Marriage and a career

By 1946, Betty also had to move out of her apartment. All her roommates were married, and she couldn't

Opposite: During World War II, the government encouraged women to help out in the aircraft industry. The U.S. Air Force needed planes for the war, but the armed forces needed the men overseas to fight the war.

"Many of us think, and I do too, that if society is to be changed, it must be done not from the top, but from the bottom."
Simone de Beauvoir, in a dialogue with Friedan in 1975

"The vote, I thought, means nothing to women. We should be armed."
Edna O'Brien, writer

23

BORN CLOTHES

This 1944 clothing advertisement shows a woman in a tailored, professional suit. But of the 33 percent of married women employed during World War II, most held factory jobs or worked as secretaries and nurses. They did not need nor could they afford such clothing.

afford the rent on her own. So she moved to a small, dark apartment in the basement of a two-family house. The apartment didn't even have a kitchen, but Betty didn't care. She rarely cooked anyway. She felt completely independent for the first time in her life.

But her independence was short-lived. A friend at work introduced her to Carl Friedan. He had run an army show in Europe for the soldiers, and he was returning to the New York area in order to open a summer theater in New Jersey. He was a promoter and full of ideas. Carl and Betty fell in love and, because apartments were so scarce, it seemed like a good idea for him to move in. In June 1947 they were married and Betty became Mrs. Carl Friedan.

Betty kept her job at the newspaper. Carl worked hard, but the theater wasn't steady work. They needed her paycheck to make ends meet.

And she was happy to keep working. The apartment didn't need her constant attention and so much was going on in the world. World War II had raised many serious political and social issues. One was the fear that communism would spread from the Soviet Union to Europe and the United States. Another was the rebuilding of Europe after the destruction caused by the war.

Living in two worlds

Betty found herself becoming more and more politically involved. She attended meetings, made speeches, heard people call her a radical, and learned that political power meant the power to make important changes that affect everyone's lives. She realized that men held all that power. Women had the right to vote, but they didn't occupy any important political positions. So they had no say in the decisions about policy. She also noticed that African-Americans and other minorities were not allowed to participate in the political process.

But her world suddenly grew smaller in 1949. That year she became pregnant and gave birth to her son, Danny. She had to take a leave of absence from her job. Her political committees suggested that it might be unseemly for a pregnant woman to be making speeches. She should be home preparing for the birth, they said. And once Danny was born, he needed all her attention.

Still, Betty did rush back to her job as soon as she could. She'd enjoyed the time at home with Danny. She loved taking care of him and watching him grow. But the newspaper needed her back. She was torn. It would be a joy to return to the business world of deadlines, debates, and writing.

But it was also a joy to watch Danny learn new things. For the first time, Friedan understood the dilemma of women who had children but also wanted to work. There were rewards at home and at work, but each reward was different, with its own benefits. Friedan didn't want to give up either one.

Room to move

But soon the choice was taken out of her hands. In 1950, Friedan was fired because she was pregnant again. The newspaper just couldn't afford to wait another year while she went on leave. Legally, they couldn't fire her. Her union contract said she was entitled to maternity leave as often as she needed it. But no amount of protest could change the editor's mind. Even Friedan's union suggested that she brought the problem on herself. After all, they said, it was her choice to get pregnant again.

Carl gave up his dream of being a theatrical producer and switched to advertising. The work was steadier and paid more. Besides, they now had a beautiful apartment with other stable families around them. It became very important to fit into the mold. Carl needed to have a serious job, and Betty needed to be a mother. Jonathan was born in 1950.

Raising two children in the city became a chore. The park was so far away and two boys needed room to run around. Friedan began to look for a house. She found an old Victorian house in Grandview, a suburb just north of New York City. The house had a huge, sloping lawn and a view of the Hudson River. It seemed like the American dream. Here the boys could stretch out and grow up without the dangers of traffic, crime, and pollution.

Building a nest

Friedan put her energies into restoring the house. She stripped all the wood trim and stairways down to their original finishes. She restored the marble fireplace, repapered the entire house, and scoured antique sales for furniture bargains. After she finished, the house looked beautiful. She felt that it was a great home for her growing family. By 1957 she and Carl would also have a daughter, Emily, to look after.

Despite all her children and all her efforts in the house, Friedan still felt dissatisfied. She missed the witty, intellectual arguments she had had at work and with members of her political committees. In Grandview, during the day, she was isolated from most outside contact. The neighborhood wives would occasionally get together, but she felt that somehow their discussions were less important and interesting than the conversations that took place in the world outside the home. She wanted to discuss world events, argue politics, and create "a work" that people other than her children and husband would notice. She quickly took stock of her situation. The house was nearly finished and the children would be in school in a few years, so she had time now to pursue these other interests.

Once again she turned to writing. While the children slept or played outside, Friedan cleared off the

Betty with Carl. Carl Friedan was a typical father of the 1950s. He spent time with the children, but left their care and discipline to Betty. She felt that this arrangement meant that men missed out on the pleasures of raising their children.

kitchen table and for a few hours made it her office. She wrote articles for women's magazines, pounding away on an old typewriter. Sometimes it took weeks to finish a short article because the children needed her attention. But she enjoyed the work and the challenge of thinking about and researching a topic. So she didn't mind how slowly the writing went. It just felt good to be doing something intellectually challenging.

Reading between the lines

Articles in women's magazines in the 1950s tried to make women feel lucky to be housewives. Editors of these magazines recognized that during World War II, women had been important members of the work force for about five years. After the war, many of them had to give way to the men returning from the war. Suddenly their status shifted dramatically. No longer in charge, they took a back seat to their husbands' careers. They were expected to stay home and raise families.

As important as that job was, for many women it didn't match the exhilaration and social involvement of their work during the war.

So the magazines worked hard to convince women that being a housewife required even more skill and intelligence than being in the work force. Women read that they were masters of many trades, while their husbands knew only a few. They read psychologists telling them that full-time mothers raised the most well-adjusted, intelligent, and capable children.

Friedan began to doubt these articles, even though she, too, wrote some of them. Certainly she loved being a mother, and she worked hard to be a good one. Yet she felt dissatisfied. At Smith College she had been considered brilliant and promising. Now she felt ordinary. Even writing her articles didn't use half the talent she developed at Smith and Berkeley. She couldn't help feeling like a failure.

Not living in anyone's shadow

One day she interviewed a woman scientist who lived in her neighborhood. This woman was developing theories about a possible new Ice Age. Friedan researched as much as she could about physics and geology before the interview, and she had to keep a

"'Occupation?' the census taker asked. 'Housewife,' I said. Gertie, who had cheered me on in my efforts at writing and selling magazine articles, shook her head sadly: 'You should take yourself more seriously,' she stated. I hesitated, then said to the census taker, 'Actually I'm a writer.'"
Betty Friedan

"Men cook more [now], and we all know why. It is the only interesting household task. Getting down and scrubbing the floor is done by women, or by women they've hired."
Nora Ephron, author

This woman points out the benefits and beauty of folding closet doors. Women were expected to be in charge of the home, so advertisers of household improvements concentrated on women buyers rather than men.

textbook open beside her as she wrote the article. She loved the challenge. More important, she began to question what she could do to fulfill the promise she'd had at Smith. If this woman scientist could have a family and still pursue her career, than Friedan knew *she* could also. She just had to find the career she wanted to pursue.

The article Friedan wrote about the scientist and her theories, "The Coming Ice Age," attracted attention. Usually Friedan wrote articles that the women's magazines felt were appropriate for *women* to read. It was believed that articles about raising children, for example, didn't concern men at all. This article didn't focus on how to be content as a housewife. This article dealt with science, a subject considered at that time to be interesting mainly to men. It explored an academic rather than a social discovery. George Brockway, an editor at a publishing company called W. W. Norton, loved the article. He wanted her to turn it into a book.

Once again Friedan found herself in a dilemma. If she wrote the book, it wouldn't really be *her* work. Instead she'd be reporting on the work of another woman. On the other hand, if she turned this opportunity down, she might never have the chance to publish anything other than "women's" articles.

After a few days, Friedan decided. For too many years she'd stood by, supporting someone else's accomplishments — her husband's work, her children's education and other activities, and the lives of people she wrote about. Now it was time to do something that was all hers. "No, thank you," she told Brockway. "If I'm ever going to write a book, it's going to be about my own work!"

But what was her work? She'd studied to be a psychologist, but she'd never practiced. She'd been a reporter, but that had been years ago. She was a mother, but writing about motherhood didn't allow her to enter the male-dominated outside world. It was so frustrating. So Friedan returned to writing articles and waited to discover what her calling would be.

American dream — or nightmare?

In 1957, some of Friedan's Smith classmates asked if she would prepare a questionnaire for the women in her

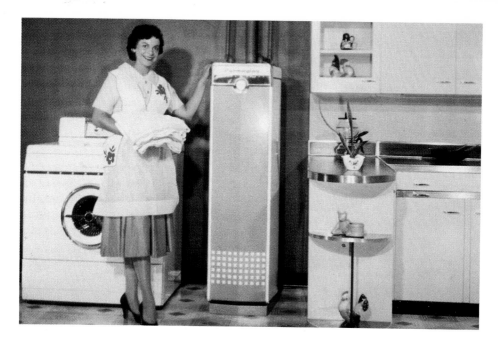

college class. They wanted to find out all the normal information. Were they married? How many children did they have? Where did they live? What had they been doing? They wanted to publish this as part of a fifteen-year reunion celebration. Friedan gladly agreed to take on the job.

But as she began to prepare the questionnaire, she thought about her own sense of failure and she wondered if other women in her class felt the same way. So Friedan designed a very different questionnaire. She asked her classmates how they felt, what bothered them, if they believed they had made use of their education, how they might do things differently if they could.

The answers were shocking. Friedan had thought this unhappiness was only her problem. She often wondered if she felt miserable because her mother had. Her neighbors hinted that they were discontent. But no one came right out and said, "I hate my life." So Friedan thought that most women were happy fulfilling the "American dream" of raising a family or happily pursuing careers, not caring about marriage. Instead, she found that most of the women from Smith were miserable.

In the 1950s, advertisers promoted modern labor-saving appliances for the home. After World War II, the American economy improved, so many families had extra money to spend. The idea of faster, fancier cleaning devices appealed to women who cared for the home. Advertisers focused their attention on these home-bound consumers.

"I prefer the word 'home-maker' because 'housewife' always implies that there may be [another] wife someplace else."
Bella Abzug, American politician

They, too, wondered why they had spent so much time preparing for an intellectual life, when they never felt that they used their knowledge. Too many career women found themselves in jobs that were reserved for women — as teachers, secretaries, and clerks — with low pay and little advancement. Women who had entered traditionally male jobs — as lawyers, engineers, and managers — found their advancement slow. They were often passed over for promotion in favor of married men who had families to support. Married women wondered why they couldn't be happy having a nice home, a successful husband, and healthy children. They thought there might be something wrong with them because they couldn't be content with the great American dream.

Emily, Friedan's daughter, benefitted from her mother's efforts. Emily went to medical school in the 1970s. In the 1960s, only 2 percent of medical school students were female. Today more than one-third of the students receiving degrees in medicine are women.

The answer to a prayer

Suddenly Friedan found a goal. She'd combine her reporting and writing skills with her psychological training to analyze and report on her results. She thought this would make a fantastic article.

She decided to concentrate on married women since she was part of this group and because in the 1950s and 1960s, the goal for most women was to get

married. There must be many other married women out there, she thought, feeling the same way as her Smith classmates did and wondering if others felt this way. Friedan hoped to make them feel better, but she also hoped to discover a solution to their misery. With great pride and anticipation, she submitted the article to her usual women's magazines.

The results shocked her. No one wanted to publish her article. The editors said it was too radical, it would stir women up, it was too negative, it presented a false view. They also feared it would anger the companies who paid millions of dollars to have their products advertised in the magazines. No publishers wanted to risk losing this important source of financial support for their magazines. Friedan went to other magazines, but no one would touch it.

One editor did like Friedan's article. He knew his magazine wouldn't publish it, but he thought her ideas were important and should be heard. He suggested she expand her article into a book. He felt that since book publishers didn't rely on advertising for support, there would be a better chance of having it published.

Finally, after twenty years, her prayer was answered. She had "a work to do."

Getting the word out

The questionnaire showed that many married women had been unhappy a long time — *and* that they felt guilty about being unhappy.

According to the media, these women had the best of lives. Situation comedies portrayed families with Father pursuing his career and Mother happy at home with the children. This seemed ideal. So, naturally, unhappy women felt that there must be something wrong with them if they weren't satisfied with home, husband, children, and relatively comfortable lives.

Betty called this the *feminine mystique*. A mystique is something accepted and even revered. Our culture reveres the roles of wife and mother, and at one time it was assumed that marriage was the only choice for a woman. Many women who accepted this mystique, however, soon found that they hungered for intellectual stimulation. Friedan called their unhappiness "the problem that has no name." Other problems — like

"Whatever women do they must do twice as well as men to be thought half as good. Luckily, this is not difficult."
Charlotte Whitton,
Canadian politician

"Each of us thought she was a freak 10 years ago if she didn't experience that mysterious . . . fulfillment waxing the kitchen floor as the commercials promised."
Betty Friedan

"I'm nasty, I'm bitchy, I get mad, but by God I'm absorbed in what I'm doing."
Betty Friedan, to reporters

31

poverty and racial and religious prejudice — had names. Social scientists studied these problems. They rarely studied the problems of middle-class women.

Betty began to understand why her mother had been so bitter. Women weren't in control of their own lives. They depended on their husbands to earn money and rarely left their own neighborhoods. Yet women had so much to offer. One thing she could offer would be her thinking about this subject.

A balancing act

Betty wanted to finish her book in a year, but she also had responsibility for the house and children. So she would steal time here and there to write, setting up the dinner table as her desk and clearing it off when it was time to serve dinner.

Writing went slowly. In time, tension increased between Betty and Carl. Writers need to spend lots of time alone, thinking and carefully wording their ideas

Friedan believed that many women would understand what she was trying to say in her book. So she traveled all over America to promote it on talk shows and in bookstores.

32

for readers. This made Betty feel even more isolated than she had been before, and the conditions under which she wrote made her envy Carl's independence. Worse, she felt that he was not concerned about her frustration. In time, Carl became less and less tolerant of her devotion to the book. And she grew more angry that Carl didn't seem to understand why she needed to take time away from her household duties to write.

Making time

Soon Friedan realized that she couldn't write the book stealing a few hours here and there. She knew that the New York Public Library had a quiet room set aside for writers. Working there would mean rushing into the city every morning and rushing home before the children got home from school. But she knew that if she didn't do this, she'd never finish the book.

On her first morning on the bus, Friedan felt both happy and sad. She felt the fun of her reporting days return and looked forward to talking with other writers. But she also knew that this time away meant upsetting Carl and spending less time with her children.

She would struggle with this dilemma often, and she knew other women must be feeling the same way. That was why it was so important to get the book written — to tell other women that they weren't the only ones who were frustrated and confused.

The Feminine Mystique

The difficulties of balancing her roles as wife, mother, and writer meant putting the writing on hold sometimes. Progress was sometimes slow, but finally, after five years, she finished the book.

When Friedan took her book to her publisher, she was astonished. He said that he didn't think it would be very important! Most women weren't as dissatisfied with being housewives as Friedan thought, he said. Besides, why would they buy this book with its confusing title by an unknown author?

So when the book finally appeared in 1963, the publisher printed very few copies. But Friedan had great faith in the importance of her work. She knew there were many women who wanted the reassurance that their feelings weren't unimportant or strange.

"I clean my own teeth. I don't ask my wife to do it."
A man from China, to Simone de Beauvoir

"There is more difference within the sexes than between them."
Ivy Compton-Burnett, English novelist

Betty felt certain that she couldn't depend on the publisher to promote her book. She had to get the word out on her own.

Making waves

So Friedan, normally shy, went on a promotional tour for her book. She spoke on women's TV shows, visited bookstores, and did interview after interview.

Women heard this provocative, if somewhat soft-spoken, author, and heard that they weren't alone in their frustrations. The book sold out in a few weeks. Friedan became even more in demand as a speaker.

Once again she faced a dilemma. If she continued to promote her book and take speaking engagements, she would be less available for her family. But if she stayed home she might never discover how much she could accomplish.

The asthma attacks returned as she tried to balance her guilt about leaving the children for her other pursuits. She and Carl had to work out compromises about housework and the children. It wasn't always easy, but by now Carl knew that Friedan had to pursue her writing and speaking.

Over three million people bought her book, but not everyone agreed with it. Friedan began to receive hate mail from men and women who thought she was upsetting an important tradition. Many career women thought she was wrong to encourage housewives to consider other paths because more women in the work force might mean less power for them.

Friedan had thought women would be glad to hear that it wasn't wrong to want more or to feel unsatisfied. She also thought that women with power would want to help other women share in that power.

Instead, some housewives worried that their husbands would now expect them to find paying jobs. Working women worried that they'd be forced to share some of the advantages they had worked hard to get.

Friedan wanted women to work together. She had to find a way for women to get together, talk, and develop common goals. The official formation of a women's organization wouldn't come for several years, but as Friedan traveled, she encouraged women to listen to one another and to find ways to help each other. Wouldn't all women benefit from higher pay in the job market? Didn't women need better legal protection when they lost their husbands through divorce or death? Weren't there a number of issues all women had a stake in?

A rising tide

Friedan wasn't the first woman to write about women's limited options. In 1949, French writer Simone de Beauvoir had published her book on women's issues, *The Second Sex.* As early as the 1950s, Gwendolyn Brooks, a black poet, had begun writing poems about black women's experiences and the injustices they suffered as African-Americans and as women.

In 1963, Gloria Steinem began exploring women's employment issues with an article exposing the exploitation of Playboy bunnies. By the late 1960s, women's magazines such as *McCall's*, *Redbook*, and *Ladies' Home Journal* began to print stories on the women's movement, as it was now being called. Friedan was asked to contribute articles, when only a few years before the same magazines had called her ideas crazy.

The more she spoke and wrote, the more women she met who felt the same way as she did. A woman

"We black women know what oppression is, what it is to be discriminated against, exploited — and that we need equality sisters of every color, all races — we can work in unity."

Dorothy Height,
African-American activist

Like Betty, poet Gwendolyn Brooks combined raising a family and writing. She won the Pulitzer Prize in poetry in 1950.

Many feminists wore this button to point out that women weren't paid as well as men for the same work. It was estimated that for every dollar that a man made, women only earned fifty-nine cents.

once wrote Friedan, "If you ever start an NAACP* for women, count me in."

Friedan had always considered herself a writer rather than an activist or an organizer. But she was hearing over and over that women didn't just want to *know* that they were frustrated — they wanted to do something about it. But what could be done?

Friedan felt it was critical that women have more choices. She also recognized the important contribution women made as mothers. She didn't hate men, as some women who now called themselves feminists did. She wanted women to have more opportunities, while still maintaining their right to be homemakers if they chose to. Still, Friedan recognized the need for a national organization to promote women's issues and keep the dialogue going that her book had begun.

Focusing on a cause

She and a few other women began to try to figure out what the most important issues were for women. They decided they were equal opportunity in employment and equal pay for equal work.

In 1964, the U.S. Congress passed a civil rights bill that banned racial discrimination in employment. In a provision that was first suggested as a joke, the law also banned sex discrimination in employment.

Even so, while it became illegal to separate job ads by headings for whites or for blacks, it was still okay to separate ads by "men's" and "women's" jobs as long as the newspaper ran a disclaimer in small print: "No advertised jobs discriminate on the basis of race or sex." Editors argued that the job headings were for the reader's convenience. Men, they argued, were seeking high-paying professional and blue-collar positions, while women sought only to pass a few hours of the day in clerical and secretarial positions.

Friedan spoke before the Equal Employment Opportunity Commission on the inequality of employment opportunities. She argued that many mothers who had no husbands needed to work to support their families. They deserved the chance to pursue the best

*National Association for the Advancement of Colored People, a civil rights organization for blacks.

jobs available. And women who worked in order to challenge themselves also deserved equal treatment. As long as the EEOC turned its back on the practice of separating jobs into male and female categories, women would find their choices and earnings limited.

Richard Graham, head of the EEOC, sympathized but had limited power to make policy changes. He could only recommend changes. As the hearings continued, Friedan knew that nothing would change unless women exerted more authority. They needed their own organization to do that.

Time for action . . . NOW!

In June 1966, on one of her frequent visits to Washington, D.C., Friedan decided it was time for action.

A crisis was occurring in employment issues. Richard Graham was not going to be reappointed to head the EEOC. President Lyndon B. Johnson considered him too sympathetic to women's rights. Also, a convention of state commissions created to study the status of women completely avoided the issue of sex discrimination in employment.

Women needed an organized force to represent them in employment issues. Friedan knew that plans must be made before she returned to New York. She invited Graham, Pauli Murray (a civil rights lawyer), Kay Clarenbach (head of the Wisconsin Commission on the Status of Women), and Dorothy Haener (a United Auto Workers member) to meet for lunch at the Washington Hilton.

Sitting around the lunch table in the crowded, noisy restaurant, they discussed the principles and goals of an organization that would be dedicated to making changes on women's issues.

They decided to call this organization the National Organization for Women — NOW. Although they concentrated on women's issues, the organizers believed that if they were to develop a strong power base, then men should not be excluded. Friedan had finally found a way for women and men with different interests and needs to get together and talk.

More important, they could decide on goals they wanted to pursue, and together they'd have enough power to get some of these goals accomplished. The

Since its adoption in 1968, NOW's logo has become one of the most widely recognized symbols in America. It appears on everything from picket signs and bumper stickers to T-shirts and buttons like this one.

"Equality for women doesn't mean that they have to occupy the same number of factory jobs and office positions as men, but just that all these posts should . . . be equally open to women."
Soviet writer and dissident Aleksandr Solzhenitsyn, in a letter to Soviet leaders

Betty is shown here at a meeting with NOW's first board chair, Kay Clarenbach.

first three hundred members were made up of women attending the convention of state commissions on the status of women. In fact, it was at the final luncheon of that convention that Friedan proposed the creation of NOW. The stated purpose of the organization was "to take the actions needed to bring women into the mainstream of American society, now, full equality for women, in fully equal partnership with men."

For the moment they agreed that they would focus their efforts toward women's employment issues — equal pay, more job opportunities, day care, and abolishing discrimination based on sex. But they also recognized that women's needs went beyond the work place. They knew that eventually, NOW would have to address other concerns.

On October 29, 1966, NOW officially began with a meeting in Washington, D.C., of thirty of the first three hundred members. They met to approve the statement of purpose and skeletal bylaws, as well as to elect the first officers.

Kay Clarenbach was elected NOW's first board chair, Friedan was elected president, Aileen Hernandez became vice president (west), and Richard Graham became vice president (east). Secretary-treasurer was Caroline Davis, of the United Auto Workers (UAW). NOW had very little money. What it had was the support of its members, both at home and at work. During off-hours, they tirelessly printed flyers and letters. *Now* they could begin to work for changes.

Help wanted

The first official act of NOW was to petition the EEOC to remove the guidelines that permitted "help wanted" advertising in newspapers to be separated into male and female categories.

Instead of several separate voices speaking before the commission, NOW carried the force of a national group of voters standing behind an issue. The officers met with President Johnson. They convinced him to include a ban on sex discrimination by federal contractors and subcontractors in an executive order. This meant that contractors who wanted to bid on federal construction projects *had* to hire women. NOW was showing the power it could exert.

As NOW accomplished more of its goals, it gained more publicity. Women and men wanted to join and to form chapters in their towns. From the beginning, NOW was meant to have strong local chapters that developed their own local goals and issues.

As a result of this growth, NOW moved beyond employment issues into areas such as abortion and birth control, discrimination in clubs, inheritance taxes, divorce, and adoption. Some of these battles made national headlines, but most were quietly fought at local levels without much publicity.

Growth and dissent

Friedan was amazed at how quickly NOW grew into an important political force. NOW pursued lawsuits in many areas where it felt women's rights were unfairly restricted. Some of these issues included civil rights violations affecting women, restrictive abortion laws, and mandatory retirement at age thirty-five for female flight attendants.

As NOW began to grow, more politicians began to respect the opinions of NOW members. Many of these politicians did not agree with the principle of women's equality, but they respected the fact that women were 53 percent of the voting public. If politicians wanted to be reelected, they knew they *had* to listen.

Of course, the more issues NOW took on, the more its membership became fragmented. Some members felt the focus should remain on employment. Others were concerned mainly about abortion.

"All the men on my staff can type."

Bella Abzug,
American politician

39

Friedan felt that after a year NOW's growth had to be considered. The board needed to address the broad range of issues that women wanted discussed, and they had to make some decisions.

"I ask," she said, speaking to the board, "for a serious respect for our differences, and for an ability to overcome our prejudices and to see beyond the moment to the future." Friedan didn't want NOW to fall apart because women had so many concerns. She wanted it to be stronger by accepting more of them.

No women allowed!

In 1964, shortly after Friedan published *The Feminine Mystique*, she had been invited to lunch at the Plaza Hotel in New York by the publisher of *New York* magazine, Clay Felker. Felker was interested in this fiery and controversial new author.

Friedan got to the hotel early, so she decided to wait in the Oak Room bar. Before she could enter, a waiter stopped her. "No, madam, you cannot wait at the bar. Women are not allowed."

Friedan was shocked. She had just finished a best-selling book about how women were second-class citizens, and here she was experiencing it. She was taken by surprise, and was at a loss for words. In disbelief, she left without a fight. But five years later she would get her revenge.

On February 12, 1969, a group of women gathered outside the Plaza to protest the Oak Room's discriminatory policy. They had agreed that a few of them would peaceably enter the room, borrowing tactics from the civil rights demonstrations. The women would seat themselves and demand service. If they were served, then the barrier was broken; if not, then they would sue.

Friedan had no idea that this would turn out to be one of the most publicized efforts of NOW up to then. She also had no idea that it would be a turning point in her own life.

When the time for the protest came, Friedan had not arrived. Her friend, Dolores Alexander, called her at home. Friedan answered.

"Why aren't you here?" Alexander demanded, with worry in her voice. "We're ready to start."

"We can say the brotherhood of man, and pretend that we include the sisterhood of women, but we know that we don't."

Germaine Greer, feminist writer, in her book The Female Eunuch

Opposite: Under Betty's aggressive leadership, NOW rapidly became an important political force for women's rights.

"I can't come," Friedan answered, far more quietly than Alexander had ever heard her.

Not come? This was an important protest. It needed the head of NOW to make it official. There were TV cameras and reporters everywhere.

But Friedan still refused. "Why?" Alexander was beginning to get angry.

Friedan reluctantly answered, "My face is all bruised and swollen. Carl hit me. We had an argument, and he hit me. It's happened before."

Alexander couldn't believe it. Friedan had never shown any sign of bruises or spoken of any trouble between her and Carl. But that is often the case with abused women. They will keep silent because they believe the abuse will end. Sometimes they are ashamed that it's happening to them. Abuse doesn't happen only to wives of alcoholics or abusers of other drugs. Abused women come from every walk of life. And Friedan was living proof of that.

But right now Friedan was as concerned about the abuse as she was about the protest. She couldn't show up bruised at a rally where television and newspaper reporters would see her.

But she needed to be there. People would wonder why the founder of NOW couldn't come to the group's first organized protest. Dolores had an idea. Could a make-up artist cover up the bruises so that Friedan could still appear? "Okay, that's a very good idea," Friedan agreed. After a tense, hour-long delay, she appeared at the Plaza.

A difficult realization

While she made it through the demonstration, she still had to deal with being a battered wife. In the 1960s, women didn't talk about being abused. If their husbands, fathers, and boyfriends became violent, they often thought that perhaps they had done something to deserve it.

Friedan had thought that way for a long time. She'd been so busy with her writing that she wondered if Carl had a right to hit her in anger because she wasn't being a "perfect" wife. But the more she talked to other women, the more she realized that no one had the right to hit another person, no matter what the frustration.

It was time for Friedan to admit that her marriage could never be perfect. But more important, she had to admit that her marriage had been based on convenience and tradition, not on shared goals and respect.

Making a tough choice

Asking for a divorce was a painful decision. Friedan knew that if she stayed home, she would be physically abused and too dependent on Carl's money to leave and save herself.

On the other hand, some people felt the women's movement was filled with "man haters" and "home wreckers." Her divorce would fuel such criticism. But Friedan knew that divorce had occurred long before the modern women's movement gained publicity. She was torn between her own needs and her desire to show NOW in a positive light.

In May 1969, Betty and Carl were divorced. The abuse and anger in their home had been too much to bear. Carl was also miserable, and Betty knew she was doing her share of adding to his misery.

Painfully, Friedan realized that she was duplicating her own parents' unhappy life. She knew that no one could rebuild a marriage when love and respect no longer existed in the home. Yet she remained disheartened by the divorce. Her children loved their father, and they would be hurt. Divorce wasn't a happy choice, but it was a necessary one. In time, the children would recover, as long as the love that did remain wasn't damaged any further.

Carl speaks out

Friedan knew her children would rebound, but she worried that she would be lonely and that the media would paint the divorce in the worst possible light. She also worried that NOW would lose important backers.

In fact, none of that happened. But Carl was angry that Betty didn't seem upset. So months after the divorce he gave an interview about what he called the "real" Betty Friedan. The interview was spiteful and cruel. He accused her of hating men, of not being a real housewife, and of acting like a little girl.

Everything Friedan had thought was behind her suddenly reappeared. She knew that Carl lashed out

"Men and women, women and men. It will never work."
Erica Jong, author

"I refuse to consign the whole male sex to the nursery. I insist on believing that some men are my equals."
Brigid Brophy, English writer

43

because he was hurt and confused, but now she had to defend herself and her cause. She spoke out in interviews. For a time it seemed the focus of the women's movement would be only on the Friedans' divorce.

Other NOW board members encouraged Friedan to find another outlet for her anger and frustration. They suggested that she continue writing the book that she had abandoned during the recent formation of NOW and her divorce from Carl. Friends also hoped she would help them advance two important causes: abortion rights and the Equal Rights Amendment.

An explosive issue

Although both of these issues aroused heated debate, the legalization of abortion was and is today an extremely emotional issue. Many men and women in America feel that abortion is wrong because they believe it destroys human life. Others believe that women should have the right to decide whether they should get an abortion or not.

In 1969, women couldn't get abortions legally unless a doctor recommended them. Often, they could be done only if the woman's life was in danger.

But women still had abortions for other reasons — reasons they thought were important even if the laws did not agree. In order to get these abortions, they would travel to other places where abortions were legal. But only the very wealthy could afford to do this. Most women had to go to illegal abortionists who often did the abortions in unsanitary conditions with dangerous equipment. Many of these abortionists weren't even doctors or nurses. They were just people who did abortions to make money. These "back alley" abortions, as they were called, were also expensive, so some women tried to do abortions on themselves. As a result, women died or permanently damaged themselves so they could no longer give birth.

This NOW button stressed that women should have the choice of a safe and legal abortion.

Coming up with a plan

NOW wanted women to have the right to choose to have safe and legal abortions. They wanted to be certain that they would be performed in sanitary medical facilities that would ensure a woman's health and safety. They argued that only women had the right to

decide what happened with their own bodies, and that included the right to abortion.

Friedan agreed, so along with other NOW board members, she organized marches and rallies to show lawmakers that many women wanted the right to safe abortions and the right to decide for themselves when to have them.

She knew that there would be great resistance. Many people believe that human life begins at conception and that abortions are wrong. They believe just as strongly in their position as NOW does in its. This would not be an easy issue to resolve. NOW even lost members over the issue, but Friedan couldn't back down. Too many women were counting on her and on NOW to make their wishes known.

First, NOW organized "speak-outs" in various cities. Here women could meet and speak out about abortion. In these meetings women who had had painful illegal abortions could share their feelings. They could join forces to battle against the laws that prohibited abortions. Many women decided to march and speak out publicly. Friedan knew that a lot of women had had illegal abortions but were too ashamed or frightened to stand up. Perhaps if they knew how large a community of women they belonged to, they

"When a man gets up to speak, people listen, then look. When a woman gets up, people look, then, if they like what they see, they listen."
Pauline Frederick (1885-1938), American actress

45

would find the courage to become politically active and take a stand.

Even if NOW lost on this issue, Friedan knew that mobilizing women and teaching them that they had political power would be valuable.

The Equal Rights Amendment

Many feminists saw the abortion issue as just a portion of a larger issue — equal rights for all people. Friedan knew that women were still far behind men in many areas. Women earned only about half of what men earned. Women were poorly represented in government and on the boards of major corporations.

Only a small percentage of women worked in traditionally male areas such as medicine and construction. And some universities were still exclusively male or female. Day care was expensive, not widely available, and often not subsidized for the poor. Women who were single parents had the greatest need for day care. But often they couldn't afford it. Many women worked in low-paying occupations that left them with barely enough money for rent, food, and transportation to and from work.

Friedan thought that if an amendment to the Constitution were passed guaranteeing equal rights for women, then women would have a legal basis on which to go to court and battle for better economic and political conditions.

But many people, both men and women, were opposed to the ERA. Some argued that women would be forced to fight in combat or that bathrooms would no longer be separated by gender. Others argued that laws to secure equal rights for women already existed. Some homemakers feared that the ERA would mean that they would have to work outside the home. Divorced women feared that alimony and child support would be eliminated. In principle, many people agreed that women deserved equal rights; they just disagreed on the method of securing them.

This button appeared everywhere during the ERA campaign of the 1970s and early 1980s. Since ERA opponents often carried "Stop ERA" signs (reminding observers of stop signs), ERA supporters began to use green signs and clothes. Green and white became the pro-ERA colors.

The ERA's long road

Friedan and NOW pushed for Congress to pass the ERA and send it to the states for final approval. NOW argued that the states and the public had the right to

The idea of an Equal Rights Amendment was not new. Such an amendment had first been proposed in 1923. But in 1972 women had the political power to finally get the amendment passed by Congress. Here Congresswomen Martha Griffiths and Bella Abzug hold a copy of the amendment that the House passed in 1971 and the Senate passed in 1972.

make a decision about the ERA. Earlier versions of the ERA had been proposed to Congress but had never been sent to the states for ratification. The last serious campaign for ratification of the Equal Rights Amendment had been in 1948. But the amendment didn't pass the Senate.

In order for an amendment to be added to the Constitution, it must first be approved by a two-thirds vote in both the House of Representatives and the Senate. Then the amendment is sent to the states, where each state legislature votes on it. This is called ratification, and three-fourths of the states, or thirty-eight out of fifty, must ratify the amendment before it can become part of the Constitution.

Betty is shown talking to news reporters about the possibility of her entering the race for president in the 1972 election.

A heated national debate

The battle for both abortion rights and the ERA would be heated and long-lasting. The issues touched on political, religious, and emotional matters. Many women found that their political beliefs conflicted with their religious beliefs. People argued at work, at home, in churches, and in the streets. The civil rights movement had stirred up people's thinking, and many felt that the women's movement was an extension of this push for the equality that the Declaration of Independence had promised two hundred years before, but hadn't yet fulfilled.

But other people felt that the women's movement

challenged the American way of life itself. They believed that if women moved into roles traditionally held by men, the family structure would disintegrate.

Friedan knew that Americans might see the ERA as a dividing amendment rather than a unifying one. Opponents of the ERA often attacked the women who supported it rather than discuss the problem of women working at low-paying jobs who couldn't earn enough to support their families.

"See," they would shout, "the ERA will lead to the breakup of the family unit. Look at Betty Friedan. She's divorced." Or they would accuse feminist writer Gloria Steinem of being antifamily because she had never married.

These opponents did not work toward providing better day care so that women who had to work outside the home could feel secure leaving their children during the day. Instead, they said that such mothers were breaking up families and allowing children to miss school.

Besides, Friedan argued, families are already suffering. Without the ERA, she and other supporters said, a single woman who headed a family could not earn enough to provide for her family.* Friedan concluded that the ERA actually supported traditional roles because it offered women respect for any choice they made. They needn't become homemakers and mothers because society expected that of them. Instead, they could choose these roles as their career.

But Friedan also knew that opponents' arguments stirred up people's fears that were difficult to combat. The ERA's ratification would require a long struggle.

A long battle

In March 1972, Congress approved the ERA and sent it to the states for ratification. People began writing to their state legislatures, either supporting or opposing the amendment. The battle also spilled into the streets, with rallies outside state capitol buildings. Opponents

During the last three or four years of the campaign, ERA supporters began wearing this button.

*Actually, the ERA would directly prohibit discrimination only in government employment. It did not apply directly to private employers. But ERA supporters believed that even if the amendment applied only to government jobs, it would improve the climate for women in private employment as well.

to the ERA came forward. Businesses such as insurance companies lobbied the legislatures, arguing that the ERA would mean higher costs to employ women at equal pay in "male" jobs, with greater risks. Higher costs might result in business failures and unemployment. The argument was effective. Some state legislators were legitimately concerned. But others feared losing valuable and wealthy contributors to their campaigns. Women didn't have the clout to fight against such persuasive and powerful opponents.

After a ten-year battle, the ERA was still three states short of ratification. In June 1982, the ERA failed to receive the approval of enough states and the deadline for ratification passed. The ERA had lost.

The Supreme Court rules on abortion

While battling for ratification of the ERA, NOW also fought for women's freedom of choice regarding abortion. This battle was fought in the courts because supporters knew that only court decisions would free doctors and clinics to publicly offer safe abortions.

Lawyers for NOW argued that denying women the right to have an abortion meant denying them their freedom of choice guaranteed by the Constitution.

In 1971, a case called *Roe* v. *Wade* appeared before the Supreme Court. In this case, a woman referred to as Jane Roe challenged the state of Texas over its law prohibiting her from having an abortion. On January 22, 1973, the Supreme Court ruled, seven to two, that Texas and Georgia could not deny a woman an abortion in the first three months of pregnancy since that denied her constitutional right to privacy. The ruling meant that the restrictive abortion laws of forty-four states were no longer in effect. Abortion was now legal.

Pulling together and apart

During these battles, Friedan began to modify her views. She wanted fewer demonstrations and more activism in legislatures and corporate boardrooms.

Women were fighting their battles in small local groups, but Friedan thought these groups, although helpful in making issues public, did little to get reforms passed. She thought that bringing together the political forces of women into a large group which could lobby for reforms would be more effective than street demonstrations. So on March 22, 1971, she gathered several powerful women together to form the National Women's Political Caucus.

Friedan also continued to exercise her abrupt and abrasive tactics. She had little patience with arguments that went nowhere or with jobs left unfinished. She also didn't like being contradicted. These traits made her both a strong leader and a dividing force. Even as she pushed ideas through and got movements going, she also alienated many supporters with her bark and her bite. But she didn't have the patience to be diplomatic. She'd waited long enough for change, and she wanted it now.

The caucus drew some criticism. Many supporters of NOW felt that the group snubbed working-class women and homemakers — who were equal members in NOW. Friedan argued that women had to use their power where they could find it. Ultimately this power would guarantee more equality for women.

So she proposed that the caucus plan a national convention where women could develop a national political platform for women's issues that the caucus could pursue. Even the critics within the movement

From left to right: Gloria Steinem, Bella Abzug, and Shirley Chisholm, with Friedan, announce the formation of the National Women's Political Caucus. This group continues to lobby politicians on women's issues.

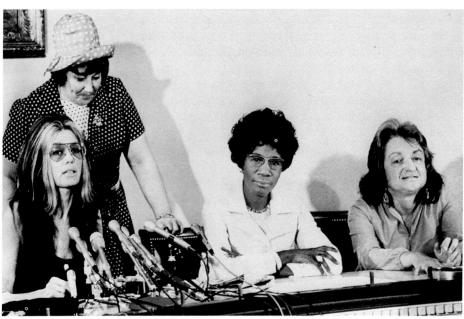

agreed that the idea of cooperation between Democratic and Republican women together to form one political platform was exciting. For the moment, Friedan's critics relented and joined in supporting her bold proposal.

Solidifying political power

On July 10, 1971, the National Women's Political Caucus convention met in Washington, D.C. Women from both major political parties, from all economic groups, and from all geographic areas met to develop a political platform which they could then promote in the upcoming presidential election.

Women met in small groups, made proposals, and then argued them out on the convention floor. The model they followed was the same one used in the Democratic and Republican national conventions. Once again, the issues deemed most important were equal rights for women, abortion rights, economic equality, and day care.

Friedan hoped to promote the platform with politicians running for local, state, and national offices. The idea was to impress politicians with the political force women could exert across party lines.

A widening gap

Friedan also began to promote an "equal partnership" between women and men in politics and at home. The more popular feminist position at the time was that women should be the leaders of the world. Women talked about other cultures which were matriarchal and argued that women would be better leaders than men because they would cooperate rather than compete.

Friedan thought such arguments offended many men and women and separated women and men even more. Proponents of these arguments said women had been offended for centuries and it was time men got a taste of their own medicine. Slowly the women's movement divided into two camps: one urging cooperation with men and one urging women's dominance.

The saving element for the movement was the fight to ratify the ERA. As long as people were working together to promote the ERA, they kept their political differences in check.

"Sometimes I thought that my main job was to keep Friedan from killing people and people from killing her."
Muriel Fox, as quoted in Marcia Cohen's The Sisterhood

"If I were a man, I would strenuously object to the assumption that women have any moral or spiritual superiority as a class, or that men share some brute insensitivity as a class. This is male chauvinism in reverse; it is female sexism."
Betty Friedan, in It Changed My Life

Friedan hoped that the women's movement would help minorities and the poor to achieve equal rights and equal pay. In 1976, Congresswoman Barbara Jordan from Texas became both the first woman and the first African-American to give the keynote address at the Democratic National Convention, held in New York City that year.

"It's a myth that women somehow need to be mothers; they no more need to be mothers than every person with vocal cords needs to be an opera singer."
Gloria Steinem

Certainly the more sensational events were being publicized. There had been a protest of the Miss America Pageant at which protesters taunted the contestants. The protesters believed that the pageant promoted the idea that women should be looked at and admired but not taken seriously. Men were barred from some feminist meetings and conferences. But most women agreed that such tactics didn't win the male political support they needed for ratification of the ERA.

Some were angry about being politically dependent on men. Friedan argued that they didn't need to be. Partnership, she said, wasn't dependence. She wanted the organized forces of women to work with the existing political forces to create an unstoppable movement for women's rights.

Criticism from the inside

The argument continued and Friedan found herself more and more in the background of the women's movement. Many feminists thought Friedan wasn't completely supportive of the movement's important issues. When Gloria Steinem founded *Ms.*, a magazine devoted entirely to feminist concerns, Friedan wasn't even part of the planning. And when Smith College chose a "Woman of the Year," it was Steinem, not Friedan, who got the honor.

Still Friedan continued to insist that women needed

to develop political cooperation with men. She felt that hating men or alienating them only put women farther away from their goal of equality with men.

In 1976, Friedan published her second book, *It Changed My Life: Writings on the Women's Movement*. In this book, she chronicled her growth as a feminist through her involvement in the women's movement and her writings about it. She wanted the book to be a history of the modern women's movement as it affected her in its first decade.

But again she received criticism.

Some women felt that the book was biased toward a moderate stance. Friedan agreed. Critics felt she should have opened the book to other writings and other points of view. But her intent was to provide a personal perspective, not a historical one.

Friedan began to teach courses in women's studies. Universities in the 1970s began to recognize the importance of the women's movement and offered courses examining the history of women in politics, literature, and social causes. Some universities offered degrees in women's studies. Friedan tried to focus on the issue of a political and gender revolution, rather than on separating women's issues from men's.

Again she came under fire. But she saw the tremendous backlash the "men-hating" speeches created. Some states had ratified the ERA and then later reversed their decision. There was even a growing movement that glorified women's submission to men.

The fruits of their labor

Despite conflicts within the movement, women were making headway. While various factions tried to work out their differences, they supported one common goal — the equal status of women.

In 1977 the leaders of the women's movement agreed that women needed an opportunity to meet without having to focus on some political battle.

The first National Women's Conference met that year. Fifteen thousand women gathered in Houston to hear speakers and discuss issues important to them. Rosalynn Carter, first lady at the time, as well as former first ladies Betty Ford and Lady Bird Johnson, attended the widely publicized conference.

"As prime minister, I'm not a woman — I'm a human being."
Indira Gandhi,
prime minister of India
(1966-77, 1980-84)

"Can't you think of another word? Feminist sounds so polarizing, so one-sexist, so anti-love?"
A young woman writing
to Ms. magazine

53

At the first National Women's Conference, women passed a lighted torch from Seneca Falls, New York — where, in 1848, the first women's rights convention had been held — all the way to Houston. Susan B. Anthony, an early fighter for women's rights, was present in 1848. Her grandniece, Susan B. Anthony II (second from left), marched the last mile to the convention hall.

There wasn't any one specific cause or political issue to be addressed. It was just an opportunity for women from all backgrounds to come together and talk. For Friedan it meant that some of the anger and division of the women's movement could be abandoned for a few days.

Moving to a second stage

Friedan continued to lecture at various universities. She focused her energies more and more on what she called "the second stage of the revolution." She argued that women needed to be outspoken and unified as a group. This allowed them to discover the issues most important to them and to make their concerns known.

But after the demonstrations and the angry protests, women now needed to work *through* the system rather than against it. Friedan believed that the earlier tactics now did more harm than good. Many men supported women's rights, and these men were often in a position to help women secure these rights. Rather than dismiss all men as foes, she suggested that men and women become allies in the struggle for equality.

In 1981, Friedan published her third book, *The Second Stage*. In it, she discussed how and why women and men should work together. She also attacked those feminist leaders who dismissed most men as unwanted and incompetent partners. She called this "female chauvinism," referring to their extreme view that females as a group were superior to males.

Friedan felt that many women were too easily dismissing men and too arrogantly promoting themselves. There had to be some middle ground.

She could look to her own two sons, Daniel and Jonathan, to know that some men were sympathetic to the problems that women faced. She believed that her sons would be good, loving husbands, willing to create a partnership with their wives.

All Friedan had ever hoped to achieve for her children, herself, and other women was the right to choose how they lived. If women were ever to be really free, they needed to invite men to join them in this freedom. Women couldn't be free if they were devoting all their energy to fighting men.

> *"Man is not the enemy here, but the fellow victim. The real enemy is women's denigration of themselves."*
> *Betty Friedan*

Benefits and battles

The women's movement has achieved much success. Attitudes have changed and some opportunities are opening up. After all, slightly more than half the people in the world are women. Government and some businesses have to be persuaded that it is wasteful to ignore the talents of all those women. They occupy many positions that had been, in the not too distant past, "for men only."

All through the 1960s, 1970s, and 1980s, Friedan had pressed for more economic and political power for women. She helped found the First Women's Bank, in New York City, a bank run by and for women. Many banks would not give women credit to borrow money for homes or cars, or for starting businesses. Friedan knew that if women couldn't control their finances, they would continually be dependent on others for support. The First Women's Bank proved that women were a good financial risk. Soon other banks began to seek women as customers.

Women are now earning almost 33 percent of all medical degrees, about 41 percent of all law degrees, and 34 percent of all business degrees. They are earning promotions in the armed forces — in some cases, becoming astronauts. They are also climbing

> *"This year women will make policy, not coffee!"*
> *Betty Friedan*

In 1963, Valentina Tereshkova of the Soviet Union became the first woman to orbit the earth during her mission on the spacecraft Vostok VI.

corporate ladders, although they sometimes find that they cannot rise to the very top. They come up against some invisible barrier. (Unlike the problem Betty Friedan wrote about, people have named this one — this barrier is called "the glass ceiling.")

Women are also moving into government at the national, state, and local levels. In the past, women have held offices, but often through what is called the "widow's mandate." This occurs when a woman's husband dies and she fills his post. Even though more women are being elected to offices in their own right, the numbers are relatively small when compared to the total number of positions held by men.

For example, there are 28 women in the House of Representatives and 2 women in the Senate, out of 535 members of Congress. Only 3 women govern states, and women legislators make up only about 17 percent, or roughly one out of six, of the total number. But these numbers, fortunately, are increasing.

New issues and renewed interest

Right now Friedan is concentrating on the women of her era — the women who first experienced independence during World War II, but then reverted to the expected roles.

Many of these women read her first book and saw their own lives in it. They set the stage for the women's movement. Now they are in their fifties, sixties, and seventies. Many are widowed or divorced.

While the women's movement takes up issues that directly affect younger women, such as abortion, equal pay, day care, and job opportunities, Friedan now concentrates upon issues affecting older women, women who are often dependent on their husbands' pensions or on Social Security. Their concern is aging. So Friedan is writing a book on aging called *The Fountain of Age*, examining how the concerns of women change with age, how women can deal with these issues, and how important the issues are to all women.

Friedan still writes and lectures, but she also has taken time to enjoy being a grandmother. She recognizes that many battles must still be fought and some battles must be refought. The abortion issue continues to divide women who struggle with the moral and

Women from Betty's generation remember when health clubs were about the only place where it was acceptable for women to take part in physical activity.

social aspects of that difficult choice. And in the work place, women still earn only about 70 percent of what men earn. That means that single mothers still often live in poverty and have difficulty offering their children opportunities to succeed.

International recognition

The United Nations set aside 1975 as "International Women's Year"; it also declared the years from 1975 to 1985 to be the "Decade of Women." The idea was to promote women's issues in an international forum.

The first international conference, in Mexico City, was somewhat disappointing. The conference was headed by Mexico's president, a man, and the speakers weren't politically powerful women in tune with the problems of the world's women.

But Friedan believed these conferences were one excellent way to focus attention on women's issues. While some feminists criticized the conferences for skirting issues that might offend some governments, Friedan felt that at least the lines of dialogue were kept open. Friedan has become an international ambassador for women's rights, visiting scores of countries. She helps women there to organize groups and teaches them techniques for lobbying their governments.

Finally having a real choice

Friedan recognizes that women today have many more options than she had when she grew up, but that they

Younger women now participate extensively in amateur and professional sports. Here, Evelyn Ashford wins the gold medal in the 100-meter run at the 1984 Olympics in Los Angeles.

The prime minister of Pakistan, Benazir Bhutto, is shown here casting her vote in her country's November 1988 general election. She is the first woman elected to govern an Islamic country.

Opposite: Many critics of Friedan thought she was too inflexible and pushy. But Friedan knew that if she didn't make waves, no one would listen and nothing would change. She thought that women had been polite and demure for too long. It was time for them to let everyone know that they wanted the chance to be more in charge of their futures and to have more choices.

also have to be true to their own desires. Choosing to be a professional might be socially acceptable now, but it may be personally unsatisfying for women who really want to be homemakers.

The point of the women's movement, Friedan continues to believe, should be that women shouldn't feel guilty about their choices and that they recognize their *own* needs.

In *The Second Stage*, Friedan wrote of "woman's need for power, identity, status and security through her own work or action in society . . . and the need for love and identity, status, security and generation through marriage, children, home, the family . . . Both sets of needs are essential to women." The women's movement has tried to make it possible for women to fulfill both needs in whatever way they feel best.

The efforts of Friedan and other important feminist leaders publicized the misery many women felt and opened up discussion that led to changes for women.

When Friedan showed women that their unhappiness and their desire to use more of their talents was shared by many other women, she motivated them to talk to one another. Even if they didn't agree on all issues, women discovered that by talking and working together, they could make important changes in their lives and in policies that affected their lives.

Friedan knows this. Women have the power to make a difference. In March 1970, Friedan left the audience at the third annual NOW convention with this remark: "I have led you into history. I leave you now — to make new history." But Betty's struggle has not ended. She continues to speak out as strongly as ever about what she believes is right — that all people deserve equal rights and equal opportunities to succeed and live fulfilling and happy lives.

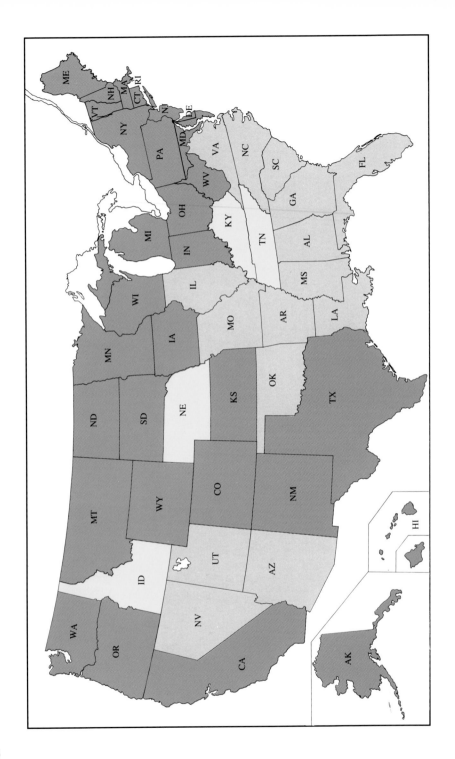

ERA RATIFICATION

The Equal Rights Amendment was sent to the states for ratification on March 22, 1972. The states shaded in green ratified the amendment on the dates listed below. The states shaded in yellow first ratified the amendment, then voted to rescind, or reverse, their decision.

State	Date of Ratification	Date Rescinded	State	Date of Ratification	Date Rescinded
Hawaii	March 22, 1972		Kentucky	June 15, 1972	1978
Delaware	March 23, 1972		Massachusetts	June 21, 1972	
Nebraska	March 23, 1972	1973	Pennsylvania	September 20, 1972	
New Hampshire	March 23, 1972		California	November 13, 1972	
Idaho	March 24, 1972	1977	Wyoming	January 24, 1973	
Iowa	March 24, 1972		South Dakota	February 2, 1973	
Kansas	March 28, 1972		Minnesota	February 8, 1973	
Texas	March 30, 1972		Oregon	February 8, 1973	
Maryland	April 4, 1972		New Mexico	February 13, 1973	
Tennessee	April 4, 1972	1974	Vermont	February 21, 1973	
Alaska	April 5, 1972		Connecticut	March 15, 1973	
Rhode Island	April 14, 1972		Washington	March 22, 1973	
New Jersey	April 17, 1972		Maine	January 18, 1974	
Wisconsin	April 20, 1972		Montana	January 21, 1974	
West Virginia	April 22, 1972		Ohio	February 7, 1974	
Colorado	April 24, 1972		North Dakota	February 3, 1975	
New York	May 3, 1972		Indiana	January 18, 1977	
Michigan	May 22, 1972				

For More Information . . .

Organizations

The following organizations can provide information about the feminist movement, the Equal Rights Amendment, the abortion issue, and other issues relating to women and women's rights. Some may have brochures or newsletters that can provide you with information. Write to them if you would like to know more about issues of interest to you. In your letter, be sure to tell them exactly what you want to know, and include your name, address, and age.

American Civil Liberties Union
132 West 43rd Street
New York, NY 10036

Anti-Defamation League of B'nai B'rith
823 United Nations Plaza
New York, NY 10013

Choice, c/o Women's Way
125 South Ninth Street, Suite 603
Philadelphia, PA 19107

Congressional Caucus for Women's Issues
2471 Rayburn House Office Building
Washington, DC 20515

League of Women Voters
1730 M Street NW
Washington, DC 20036

The Ms. Foundation for Women
370 Lexington Avenue
New York, NY 10017

National Committee for a Human Life
    Amendment
1430 K Street NW, Suite 800
Washington, DC 20005

National Foundation for the Study of
    Equal Employment
1015 15th Street NW
Washington, DC 20005

National Organization for Women
1000 16th Street NW, Suite 700
Washington, DC 20036

National Right to Life
    Committee
419 Seventh Street NW, Suite 402
Washington, DC 20004

National Women's Hall of Fame
P.O. Box 335
Seneca Falls, NY 13148

National Women's Political Caucus
1275 K Street NW, Suite 750
Washington, DC 20005

Pro Choice Defense League
131 Fulton Avenue
Hempstead, NY 11550

Planned Parenthood Federation
    of America
810 Seventh Avenue
New York, NY 10019

United Nations Development Fund
    for Women
Two United Nations Plaza
Room DC-1002
New York, NY 10017

Women's Research and Education
    Institute
204 Fourth Street SE
Washington, DC 20003

Books

The following books will give you more information about Betty Friedan, feminist issues, historically influential women, and the history of the feminist movement.

About Betty Friedan —

Betty Friedan. Justine Blau (Chelsea House)
Betty Friedan: A Voice for Women's Rights. Milton Meltzer (Penguin)

About feminism —

Feminism. Miriam Schneir, editor (Random House)
Feminism: Opposing Viewpoints. Andrea Hinding, editor (Greenhaven)
Women for Human Rights. Marcia Conta (Raintree)
Women in History. Jerry Aten (Raintree)
Women in Politics. Sharon Whitney and Tom Raynor (Franklin Watts)
Women in Power. Ginny McReynolds (Raintree)
Women Shaping History. Denise DeClue (Raintree)
Women Win the Vote. Betsy C. Smith (Silver Burdett)
Women, Work, and Wages. Gilda Berger (Franklin Watts)

About abortion —

Abortion: Facing the Issues. Susan N. Terkel (Franklin Watts)

Glossary

abortion
The deliberate ending of a pregnancy before birth. In most states, the law requires that most abortions be done in the first three months of the pregnancy. Opponents of abortion argue that human life begins at the moment of conception.

affirmative action
The practice of awarding a certain number of jobs to women or minorities even if their qualifications are slightly lower than those of other applicants. The idea behind this is that minorities and women have often been excluded from certain jobs because of unfair hiring practices or lack of educational opportunities.

anti-Semitism
Prejudice or hostility toward people of the Jewish faith because of their beliefs and cultural background. The term comes from the word *Semite,* which refers to the people thought to be descended from Noah's oldest son, Shem. In modern times, this term refers mainly to Jews and Arabs. In ancient times, *Semites* also referred to Assyrians, Babylonians, Phoenicians, and other eastern Mediterranean peoples.

asthma
A disease which makes it difficult for a person to breathe. Asthma is considered a chronic disease because it usually affects a person over a long period of time.

Asthma attacks are sometimes brought on by stress or tension. In Friedan's case, her asthma attacks occurred during times of uncertainty and indecision.

blue-collar
A term that refers to jobs that involve manual or physical labor. Some examples of blue-collar jobs include construction work, factory work, firefighting, and truck driving.

chauvinism
The belief that one's own group is better than any other. The feminist movement used the term *male chauvinist* to describe men who claimed that women were inferior to men.

enfranchisement
The giving of full rights of citizenship to a group of people. Usually this term means granting the right to vote. Women also use the term to mean equal rights on the job and under the law.

Equal Rights Amendment (ERA)
This proposed amendment to the Constitution was approved by Congress in 1972. The amendment declared that no person could be denied equal legal rights because of gender. Congress originally allowed seven years for the states to ratify the ERA. In 1978, it granted a three-year extension. In 1982, the proposed amendment still fell three states short of the necessary approval of three-fourths of the states (thirty-eight of fifty).

feminism
The idea that women should have the same political, economic, and social rights as men. This term also refers to the movement that seeks to put these ideas into practice. (*See also* **women's liberation movement**.)

gender
The classification of a person as male or female; a person's sex. Many people believe that certain attitudes and behavior can be assigned to one gender or another, and they discriminate on the basis of these beliefs. For this reason, there are many court cases brought by people who feel they have been treated unfairly as a result of their gender. One term commonly used for this type of unfair treatment is *gender bias*. (*See also* **sexism**.)

Great Depression
A worldwide economic and social crisis of the 1930s that started with the stock market crash of 1929. By 1933, 16 million people — one-third of the labor force — were unemployed.

Holocaust
With a capital *H*, *Holocaust* refers to the slaughter of 6 million Jews that occurred in Europe from 1933 to 1945, especially in Germany and Poland. Jews were rounded up and sent to concentration camps, where many were killed. The rest labored in the camps and often died of starvation or disease. With a lowercase *h*, *holocaust* refers in general to massive slaughter and destruction of life.

matriarchy

    A group or society that is run by women. Some feminists feel that societies in which women hold all positions of power are preferable to societies that are primarily run by men.

Ms.

    A title for women, similar to *Mr.,* that does not indicate a woman's marital status. Often women looking for jobs found that they were discriminated against if they were married because employers thought they would leave to have babies. Or they were discriminated against if they were unmarried because employers thought they might leave to get married.

mystique

    A set of mystical beliefs about a person, thing, or idea. Friedan argued that women became victims of a mystique that glorified housekeeping and child rearing and made staying at home seem like the only good choice for women. This caused some women to wonder why they were often unhappy doing a job that society told them was completely fulfilling.

ratification

    The approval of a constitution or an amendment to a constitution. Ratification of an amendment to the United States Constitution requires passage by three-fourths of the states. Today, that is thirty-eight states. Only thirty-five states ratified the ERA, so it did not become part of the Constitution.

sexism

    Gender bias; the treatment of one gender as more important or better than the other, or the defining of an individual by sexual stereotypes. For example, women have often been excluded from certain jobs because some people think that they are more emotional than men. (*See* **gender**.)

suffrage

    The right to vote. Women called "suffragists" began campaigning as early as 1848 to gain the right to vote. They finally won it with the passage of the Nineteenth Amendment in 1920.

white-collar

    A term that refers to jobs or professions that do not involve manual labor. Some examples of white-collar jobs include office work, teaching, sales, and government work.

women's liberation movement

    A political and social movement of the 1960s and the 1970s which wanted to change the way society viewed and treated women. These changes involved economic and educational gains, such as allowing women to enter schools and compete for jobs they had previously been barred from. The movement also sought to change the stereotypes of women in advertisements, literature, movies, and other forms of mass communication.

Chronology

1916   Jeanette Rankin becomes the first woman elected to Congress.

1920   **August 26** — The Nineteenth Amendment gives women the right to vote.

1921   **February 4** — Bettye Goldstein is born in Peoria, Illinois.

1938   Betty graduates from high school and enters Smith College in Massachusetts, where she studies psychology and edits the college newspaper.

1939   Adolf Hitler invades Czechoslovakia and Poland. World War II begins.

1941   **December** — The United States enters World War II. Many men are drafted into the armed forces, and increasingly women take their places in the factories and in other jobs.

1942   **June** — Betty graduates from Smith with honors. She goes to the University of California at Berkeley to begin work on a master's degree.

1943   Betty refuses a doctoral fellowship in psychology and moves to New York City. She gets a job as a reporter for Federated Press.
Betty's father, Harry Goldstein, dies.

1947   **June** — Betty marries Carl Friedan.

1949   The Friedans' first son, Danny, is born.
The Second Sex, by Simone de Beauvoir, is published in France (the English translation appears in 1953).

1950   Carl and Betty's second son, Jonathan, is born.

1957   Emily, their daughter, is born.
Betty prepares a questionnaire for a class reunion at Smith. "The Togetherness Woman," her resulting article, is rejected by all the women's magazines she submits it to.

1958   Friedan's article "The Coming Ice Age" is published in *Harper's.* At the suggestion of George Brockway of W. W. Norton, she begins turning her rejected article into a book.

1963   **February** — Friedan publishes *The Feminine Mystique.*
May — Gloria Steinem publishes "I Was a Playboy Bunny."
June — Valentina Tereshkova becomes the first woman in space.

1964   Congress passes the Civil Rights Act of 1964; one provision forbids sex discrimination in employment in businesses with twenty-five or more employees.

1966   **June 29** — Friedan and other women and men found the National Organization for Women (NOW) at the Washington Hilton.

1967   NOW pickets the *New York Times* against its separate "male" and "female" employment ads. The group announces its support of legalized abortion.

1968	Shirley Chisholm becomes the first African-American woman elected to Congress. Feminists picket the Miss America Pageant.
1969	**February 12** — NOW protests the "males only" policy of the Oak Room in the Plaza Hotel in New York City. Women enter the room and wait to be served during the lunch hour.
1970	**August 26** — The fiftieth anniversary of women's suffrage. A "Women's Strike for Equality" takes place nationally. Friedan leads a march down Fifth Avenue in New York City.
1971	Friedan helps organize the National Women's Political Caucus. The Supreme Court rules that women with young children cannot be denied jobs for that reason unless the same rule is applied to men.
1972	The first issue of *Ms.* magazine is published. **March 22** — The Equal Rights Amendment (ERA) is sent to the states for ratification. Twenty-two states vote for ratification by the end of the year.
1973	**January 22** — The Supreme Court rules in *Roe* v. *Wade* that denying any woman an abortion in the first trimester of pregnancy violates women's constitutional rights. Abortion thus becomes legal in the United States. Eight more states ratify the ERA; one state rescinds its ratification.
1974	Three more states ratify the ERA; a second state rescinds its ratification.
1975	The United Nations declares 1975 to be "International Women's Year," and 1975 to 1985 to be the "Decade of Women." The first world conference on women, sponsored by the United Nations, is held in Mexico City. Another state ratifies the ERA.
1976	Friedan publishes *It Changed My Life*.
1977	**November 18-21** — The first National Women's Conference is held in Houston, Texas. Three first ladies — Rosalynn Carter, Betty Ford, and Lady Bird Johnson — attend. A final state votes for ERA ratification; a third rescinds.
1978	Congress extends the deadline for ERA ratification to June 30, 1982.
1981	Friedan publishes *The Second Stage*. Judge Sandra Day O'Connor becomes the first woman to serve on the Supreme Court.
1982	**June 30** — The Equal Rights Amendment fails to achieve ratification.
1984	Geraldine Ferraro is selected by Democratic presidential nominee Walter Mondale to be his running mate and becomes the first woman to be a major-party candidate for vice president.
1989	The Supreme Court gives states more leeway in restricting abortions.

Index